June 20, 2010

To Our Son David,

    May you tre____
as you reflect _____
founding of our _____ that
we have been Blessed by God to
be a part of ~ and "We The People"
who need to continue to keep it
a Free and Strong nation for our
Children and Grandchildren.

        With Our Love,
              Mom and Dad

This signed edition of

ABRAHAM LINCOLN'S

Gettysburg Address

ILLUSTRATED

has been specially bound by the publisher

Jack E. Levin

Jack E. Levin

Mark R. Levin

Mark R. Levin

ABRAHAM LINCOLN'S

Gettysburg
Address

ILLUSTRATED

Conceived and Designed by

Jack E. Levin

Preface by

Mark R. Levin

Threshold Editions

NEW YORK LONDON TORONTO SYDNEY

Threshold Editions
A Division of Simon & Schuster, Inc.
1230 Avenue of the Americas
New York, NY 10020

First Threshold Editions hardcover edition May 2010

THRESHOLD EDITIONS and colophon
are trademarks of Simon & Schuster, Inc.

For information about special discounts for bulk purchases,
please contact Simon & Schuster Special Sales at
1-866-506-1949 or business@simonandschuster.com.

The Simon & Schuster Speakers Bureau can bring authors
to your live event. For more information or to book an event
contact the Simon & Schuster Speakers Bureau at
1-866-248-3049 or visit our website at www.simonspeakers.com.

Manufactured in the United States of America

1   3   5   7   9   10   8   6   4   2

ISBN 978-1-4391-8896-5
ISBN 978-1-4391-8900-9 (ebook)

Dedicated to my wife, Norma, and our family,
and to all the patriots who love our country

Preface

My Father and
the Gettysburg Address

On July 4, 1937, my father, Jack, then twelve years old, and a neighborhood buddy walked several miles from their homes to the parade route where the city of Philadelphia was celebrating our nation's founding. The route stretched from Center City Philadelphia, not far from Independence Hall, to the Philadelphia Art Museum, which Sylvester Stallone would make famous in his Rocky movies nearly forty years later.

One of the dignitaries in the parade caught my father's attention—a Civil War veteran. He sat on the back of a four-door convertible dressed in his old Union uniform, including his campaign hat. Behind him marched a small group of Spanish-American War veterans. But of all the soldiers, veterans, and marching bands my father saw that day, the Union soldier stood out. Young Jack had read somewhat about the Civil War in school, but seeing that soldier in the flesh intrigued him. The soldier would become seared in my father's mind. The most costly war in American history had become real to him. Thus began my father's lifelong journey of self-education and patriotic preaching about this great nation's history and founding principles.

At a young age, Jack had a knack for drawing, designing, and inventing. When he was thirteen, he designed an "automobile window" invention for a contest the *Philadelphia Daily News* was conducting in conjunction with the release of the movie *Young Tom Edison,* starring Mickey Rooney. He was one of only five winners citywide and earned a trip to the 1939 New York World's Fair. At fifteen, my father submitted an idea (with drawings) for animating the story "A Christmas Carol" to the Walt Disney Studio in California. The studio loved it and asked that he provide more examples of his work, including humorous cartoon drawings, which he did. They next contacted Jack's parents and asked whether they would allow their son to join Disney Studio. They would provide him with dormitory space and schooling at their facility while he was working for them. But his parents, concerned about his age, turned down the offer.

My father grew up during the Great Depression. His family was very poor. His father, Harry, worked at part-time jobs when he could find them. And his mother, Sarah, worked in a cigar factory. Jack was the eldest of four children, and the only boy. When he turned sixteen, after the school day ended he would walk to the cigar factory, where he worked until midnight, earning the going rate of seventeen dollars a week. On the weekends, my father took freelance jobs with furniture frame manufacturers, sketching frames to upholster sofas and chairs. He was paid two dollars for a set of three drawings. The manufacturers' salesmen used the finished drawings with their customers.

A few months later, the Japanese attacked Pearl Harbor. Jack spent the summer working at the Cramps Shipyard, where they built destroyers and submarines. But he wanted to do more for the war effort. Like so many wonderful young men at the time, my father decided to enlist in the armed forces. He wanted to be a cadet in the Army Air Corps, which today we know as the Air Force. But Jack was only seventeen. He was too young. So he secured a copy of his birth certificate from city hall and rubbed out the "5" in 1925 (his birth year) and wrote in "4." Just like that, he had reached the legal age requirement of eighteen. Now, if he could pass the rigorous Air Corps exam, he was in. Ten would-be cadets took the exam, including students from the University of Pennsylvania, but only four passed, including my father. Not long thereafter, as my father was boarding a train to Biloxi, Mississippi, for basic training, a soldier stopped him and told him the lieutenant wanted to see him. The lieutenant, who had taken a close look at the birth certificate, asked Jack how old he was. Jack told him the truth. The lieutenant wasn't very happy, but he told my father when he turned eighteen, he could join up. A week after he turned eighteen, he did. And while in the service, Jack would use brief respites to draw cartoons, which were published in a variety of newspapers.

After the war, my father worked for a company making displays for store windows and trade shows. Around this time he met a beautiful young lady, Norma Rubin. The next morning Jack told his mother that one day he would marry her. Norma headed to Syracuse University, and so did Jack, with the help of the G.I. Bill. He earned his room and board by working in the cafeteria. But Jack's love of art and history would lure him back to his hometown of Philadelphia. And after much pleading by Jack, Norma returned with him. They were soon married.

Norma was a brilliant student. She graduated from Arcadia University with a Bachelor of Science degree and began teaching fourth and fifth graders in public school. Jack enrolled in the Philadelphia College of Art, where he majored in advertising and began experimenting with new ideas, in particular unique drawings and images of clowns. He created a new concept at the time—using only hands and faces to convey ideas and messages, which he turned into a cartoon strip called, remarkably enough, *Hands and Faces*. The comic strip was so original that it was picked up by General Features Syndicate and published in newspapers throughout the United States.

It was now the mid-1950s. My parents, who were always independent and entrepreneurial at heart, decided to start their own small business—a preschool and summer day camp they named Hawthorne Country Day School and Camp. They had little money. They couldn't afford an architect to design the facilities. But like millions of others who pursued the American dream before them and since, they had initiative and ingenuity and were willing to work as hard as they needed to succeed. Norma developed the curriculum for the preschool, hired a teacher to assist her, and oversaw everything from the meals to clean-up. For the camp, she interviewed and hired the counselors, enrolled the children (ages 3 to 14 years), published a weekly newsletter, and handled all the other details required of a well-functioning program.

Among my father's first projects was to install a steel flagpole on the grounds. He wanted the American flag to be seen from all corners of the property and beyond. During camp each morning, every camper and staffer would say the Pledge of Allegiance in unison, and watch as the flag was raised in the morning, lowered at the end of the day, and meticulously folded and put away. Jack never wavered from this practice. No one was prouder to be an American.

Jack designed the school building, which was part living quarters for the family and part classrooms for the preschool. He also designed and built the wooden desks and chairs and even the wooden toys, handled all maintenance, and helped pick up the children early in the morning and drive them home in the evenings. As the school and camp grew, my father designed a second facility that included two swimming pools. My parents worked sixteen-to-twenty-hour days. Jack eventually had to drop his comic strip, which had run for three years.

In the meantime, in 1955 Norma gave birth to her first baby, Doug. He was followed by me, in 1957, and Rob, in 1958. The three sons grew up in this loving, nurturing, and often hectic environment. I remember the baseball and volleyball games, the swimming races, the donkey rides, the hiking trips, and the great lunches, especially the spaghetti and meatballs. As we boys got older, one of us would accompany my father from time to time when he would pick up the campers in the morning. We usually stopped at a favorite donut shop on the way. And on the return ride after camp, we often went to the local Dairy Queen and maybe the driving range to hit a bucket of golf balls. Despite the great joy, after nearly twenty years of grueling hours, my parents sold their beloved Hawthorne.

Even with the passage of much time, that Union soldier my father had seen on July 4, 1937, remained prominent in his memory. Jack had become somewhat of an expert on American history, constantly researching and reading about the American experience. And the more he learned, the prouder he became. He also believed it was essential that citizens, especially young people, grasp the significance of the Civil War, the unparalleled leadership of Abraham Lincoln, and the unimaginable sacrifice of hundreds of thousands of Americans in the preservation of liberty and our republic. In the early sixties, on the hundredth anniversary of the Civil War, Jack decided the moment was right to create a book about Lincoln's Gettysburg Address, one of the most historically significant speeches ever delivered by any head of state. But my father did not want to produce another text on Gettysburg or Lincoln's speech, as many outstanding texts already existed. Instead, he believed that by using his design and artistic skills, combined with the most compelling photographs of the Civil War, he could make that solemn day real, just as that Union soldier had made the Civil War real for him as a youngster.

Jack searched for the best period illustrations and battlefield images available by the most renowned photographers of the Civil War period, including Matthew Brady. He also unearthed extraordinary drawings of the nation's founding, maps, paintings, and old news articles. He sorted through them all, carefully selecting the most striking illustrations and photographs for his book. As there were no computers, he had a local printer reproduce them. Jack then painstakingly applied the Letraset lettering—which consisted of transferable letters on dry sheets of paper—to each image by hand-rubbing one letter at a time onto the images. Every page was meticulously designed. And every page was its own work of art. It was as if my father's vast historical knowledge and extensive art and design work, learned and experienced over several decades, had come together in his book.

Jack gave his book a simple title: *Abraham Lincoln's Gettysburg Address Illustrated.* And he designed the cover as well—with the colors red, white, and blue boldly displayed. He would have it no other way. The first publisher to whom he showed his book was bowled over. In 1965, they published ten thousand copies, a large number for a first-time author, which sold commercially in bookstores throughout the country. My father never created another book. He had already accomplished something few others ever would. He quietly continued to work hard at the preschool and camp, and later in a small retail shop that my parents would open in the 1970s. That's my dad.

Jack is now eight-five years old. He lives in Florida with my mother. They have been married for fifty-nine years. He continues to draw and paint. These days he is experimenting with expressionism and abstract art.

He also likes to paint Native Americans, particularly proud and dignified old warriors. Every now and then, he displays his artwork at local shows. But my father remains intensely interested in America's well-being. Each night, after the conclusion of my radio broadcast, he calls me to talk a few minutes about the issues of the day. Like millions of others, my father is concerned about the state of the nation. He wonders whether the liberty, opportunities, and prosperity fought for and enjoyed by his generation and past generations will survive for future generations.

Not too long ago, my father sent me a Xerox copy of his book, which he had reduced to a smaller size. He said, "Mark, I created this book forty-five years ago to remind people, especially young people, how precious our republic is. This might be a good time to remind them again." He was right. With the exception of improvements to the clarity and color of the graphics with digital technology, slight modifications to certain pages and the cover, and the reduced physical size of the book, *Abraham Lincoln's Gettysburg Address Illustrated* remains the same as when it was first released in 1965. But its message is all the more important.

I also want to acknowledge my brothers, Doug and Rob, who contributed to this preface by allowing me to tap their collective memories. They were always smarter and more knowledgeable than I, which they demonstrated most evenings around the dinner table, where we debated everything from history and economics to sports and politics. And I suppose I should finally admit that they were better athletes as well—Doug excelled at boxing and Rob at baseball and soccer. But today I have the microphone!

Mark R. Levin

Leesburg, Virginia

Foreword

On July 1, 1863, the Army of Northern Virginia, commanded by General Robert E. Lee, and the Army of
the Potomac, commanded by General George Gordon
Meade, met at Gettysburg, then a sleepy Pennsylvania village. Three days of bloody fighting resulted
in 28,000 Confederate and 23,000 Union dead and
wounded. The fighting was climaxed by the gallant but
futile Pickett's Charge, in which 15,000 Confederate

soldiers were repulsed at the moment of breaching the Union lines. The defeated Confederate army withdrew and retreated south. This was the last major attempt to invade the North by a Confederate Army.

Ceremonies were held at the site on November 19, 1863, to dedicate a portion of the battlefield as a national cemetery for the soldiers, both Northern and Southern, who had fallen there. After the bands had played and the dignitaries were introduced, Lincoln listened as Edward Everett, the greatest public speaker of his time, enthralled the crowds with a two-hour oration. When Everett finished, Lincoln, who had been invited to give "a few appropriate remarks," rose and delivered the Gettysburg Address.

Lincoln thought the speech a failure, but Everett was to write Lincoln the following day, "I should be glad, if I could flatter myself that I came as near to the central idea of the occasion, in two hours, as you did in two minutes."

As far as we now know, Lincoln actually wrote five copies of the Gettysburg Address in his own hand. Each was slightly different in content. The first copy, the Hay version, he wrote in Washington before going to Gettysburg. The second, the Nicolay version, and the one he supposedly used at the dedication ceremonies, was written while at Gettysburg. The third, the Everett version, he wrote at the request of Edward Everett in February 1864. That same month George Bancroft asked President Lincoln for still another copy, which was to be published in a booklet edited by John P. Kennedy and Colonel Alexander Bliss.

Lincoln sent the fourth, or Bancroft, version to Bancroft on February 29. Having written it on both sides of the paper, the copy was not suitable for reproduction, so Lincoln sent a second copy, permitting Bancroft to keep the first one. This last copy was kept by Colonel Bliss and is known as the Bliss version.

Some historians believe that Lincoln wrote and sent a copy of his address to Judge David Wills, of Gettysburg, but the Wills copy has never been found and therefore cannot be authenticated at this time. The last, the fifth, Bliss or Baltimore version, was used for this book because it is the only one of the five that shows the signature of Lincoln and the date the address was delivered. Also, it is considered to be the version probably most accurate in content to the address as Lincoln actually delivered it at Gettysburg.

In this book, a selected few from the hundreds of remarkable photographs taken by the Civil War photographers Matthew Brady, Alexander Gardner, and their peers are used as graphic complements to the words of the Gettysburg Address. It is my hope that the stark realism of these pictures, with Lincoln's words, will give readers a sense of intimacy with the events of which Lincoln spoke at Gettysburg.

Jack E. Levin

Philadelphia

ABRAHAM LINCOLN'S

Gettysburg
Address

ILLUSTRATED

JULY

4, 1776.

Four score and seven years ago,

Our fathers
brought forth
upon
this continent,

a new nation,

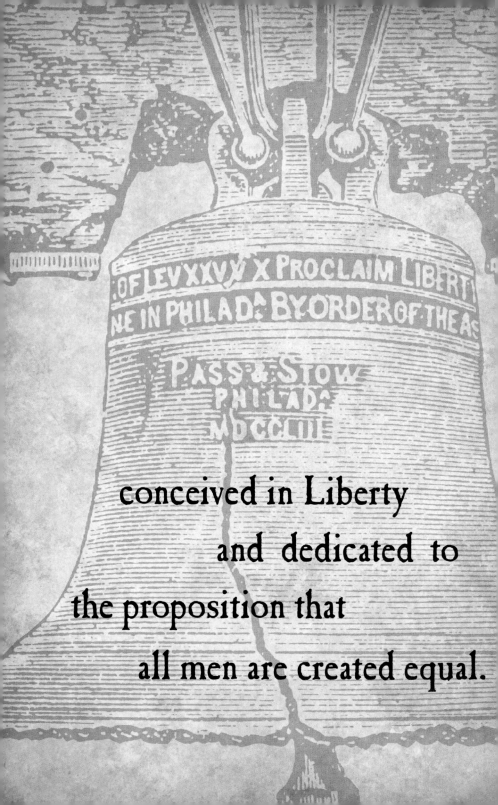

conceived in Liberty
and dedicated to
the proposition that
all men are created equal.

In CONGRESS, July 4, 1776.

The unanimous Declaration of the thirteen united States of America,

Now we are engaged

CHARLESTON

MERCURY

EXTRA:

Passed unanimously at 1.15 o'clock, P. M. December 20th, 1860.

AN ORDINANCE

To dissolve the Union between the State of South Carolina and other States united with her under the compact entitled " The Constitution of the United States of America."

We, the People of the State of South Carolina, in Convention assembled, do declare and ordain, and it is hereby declared and ordained,

That the Ordinance adopted by us in Convention, on the twenty-third day of May, in the year of our Lord one thousand seven hundred and eighty-eight, whereby the Constitution of the United States of America was ratified, and also, all Acts and parts of Acts of the General Assembly of this State, ratifying amendments of the said Constitution, are hereby repealed; and that the union now subsisting between South Carolina and other States, under the name of "The United States of America," is hereby dissolved.

THE

UNION

IS

DISSOLVED!

in a great civil war,

testing whether that nation, or
so dedicated

any nation so conceived and
can long endure.

We are met on a great battlefield of that war.

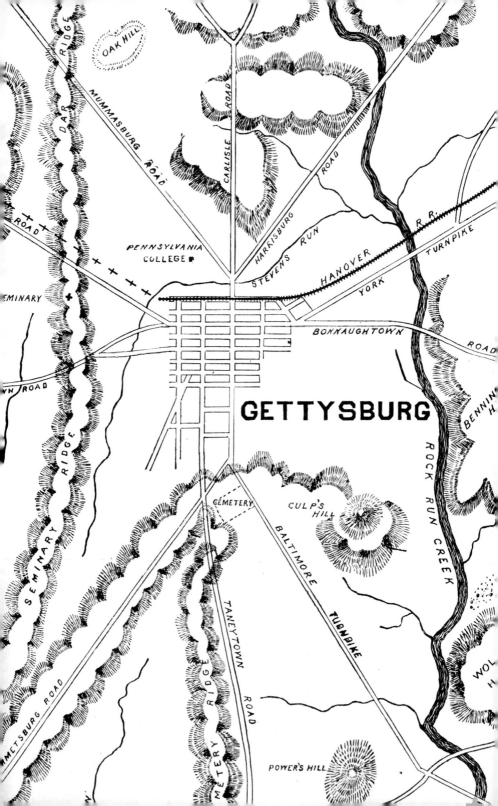

We have come to dedicate
as a final resting place
their lives that that

a portion of that field,
for those who here gave
nation might live.

It is altogether fitting and

proper that we should do this.

But in a larger sense, we can not
consecrate—we can not hallow
living and dead who struggled
far above our poor power

dedicate—we can not
—this ground. The brave men
here have consecrated it,
to add or detract.

The world will little note nor

long remember what we say here,

but it can never forget
what they did here.

It is for us the living, rather, to be dedicated here to the unfinished work which they who fought here have thus far so nobly advanced.

It is rather for us to be here dedicated to the great task remaining before us—that from these honored dead we take increased devotion to that cause for which they gave the last full measure of devotion—

ULYSSES S. GRANT
Commander of Union Armies

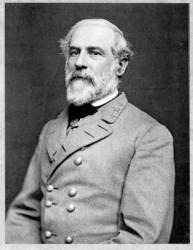

ROBERT E. LEE
Commander of Confederate Armies

2d Edition.

LEE SURRENDERS

Glory to God in the Highest:

Peace on Earth, Good will

Amongst Men.

McLean House, Appomattox Court House, Virginia

that we here highly resolve
that these dead shall not
have died in vain——

that this nation, under God, shall

have a new birth of freedom——

. . . with malice toward none;
with charity for all; with
firmness in the right, as God
gives us to see the right, let us
strive on to finish the work
we are in; to bind up the
nation's wounds, to care for
him who shall have borne the
battle, and for his widow and
his orphan—to do all which
may achieve and cherish
a just and a lasting peace,
among ourselves, and with all
nations.

—from LINCOLN'S SECOND INAUGURAL ADDRESS

and that this government of the people, by the people, for the people, shall not perish from the earth.

Address delivered at the dedication of the Cemetery at Gettysburg.

Four score and seven years ago our fathers brought forth on this Continent, a new nation, conceived in Liberty, and dedicated to the proposition that all men are created equal.

Now we are engaged in a great civil war, testing whether that nation, or any nation so conceived and so dedicated, can long endure. We are met on a great battle-field of that war. We have come to dedicate a portion of that field, as a final resting place for those who here gave their lives, that that nation might live. It is altogether fitting and proper that we should do this.

But, in a larger sense, we can not dedicate— we can not consecrate— we can not hallow— this ground. The brave men, living and dead, who struggled here, have consecrated it, far above our poor power to add or detract. The world will little note, nor long remember what we say here, but it can never forget what they did here. It is for us the living, rather, to be dedicated here to the unfinished work which they who fought here have thus far so nobly advanced. It is rather for us to be here dedicated to the great task remaining before us — that from these honored dead we take increased devotion to that cause for which they gave the last full measure of devotion — that we here highly resolve that these dead shall not have died in vain — that this nation, under God, shall have a new birth of freedom — and that government of the people, by the people, for the people, shall not perish from the earth.

Abraham Lincoln.

November 19. 1863.

Picture Credits